WASTED FAITH

WASTED FAITH

Jim Elliff

Christian Communicators Worldwide

TABLE OF CONTENTS

A VERY REAL CONCERN

Chapter 1

Most people will spend far more time examining the vegetables in the supermarket than they will ever spend scrutinizing their faith. In the following pages we will take a hard look at faith . . . *your* faith. We will pry off the lid of deceptive faith and smell its contents. In the process, we will come to an understanding of what is authentic—the faith that is the acceptable response to the activity of God. And we will discover the disturbing possibility that what we thought was conversion to Christ may have only been a shadow, an illusion, a mere experience.

Why would I encourage skepticism about your faith? The reason is perhaps too obvious to say: Deception is the eager companion of the easily convinced. Those who are *too* easily assured, who will not trouble with investigation, are likely to discover too late that they own a cheap imitation of the real. They may be like the man in Jesus' parable of the wedding feast who was cast out because he did not have the proper wedding clothes (see Matthew 22:1-14).

The person with an experience alone to validate his eternal state is in a most serious condition.

The one who says, "I know I'm a Christian because I prayed the sinner's prayer," and who believes all subsequent doubts are attacks from the enemy, is not using a biblical pattern of thinking. Such a person may be strolling precariously along the lip of hell.

Faith must have a distinct beginning in each genuine Christian life. The Scriptures repeatedly emphasize this. One moment an individual does not believe (trust, have faith—this is the meaning of the word). The next moment (although the exact point in time is not always discernible) the same person is a believer. Biblically-based Christians have always accepted this. But external acts that are considered by many to clearly mark the beginning point of faith (specifically-worded prayers, physical responses to gospel invitations, etc.) often prove to be misleading. And the deception grows stronger when the person is confidently assured by well-meaning friends or Christian leaders that his response or prayer *definitely* marks the beginning of his or her life as a Christian.

Regardless of what others may have told you about the significance of an event in your past, let me ask you a searching question: *Right now*, is your faith authentic or counterfeit? Stop and think this through. Paul did not write the following words to admitted unbelievers but to professing Christians—people like you and me. He warns:

> Examine yourselves as to whether you are in the faith. Test yourselves. Do you not know yourselves, that Jesus Christ is in you?—unless indeed you are disqualified (2 Corinthians 13:5).

We are obeying God by reexamining the issue of our own salvation. We are also acting with the highest level of common sense, considering the stakes. Will you search it out? What is most alarming is the risky willingness of many professing Christians to gamble eternity on an emotional one-time experience, a "sinner's prayer" properly prayed, or a feeling of substantial relief at a juncture in time, without ever taking a serious look at what is evident now, at this moment. Is eternal life of so little value that it seems unnecessary to examine yourself for evidence of it? Is there nothing to lose? Hell is engorged with people who once thought of themselves as Christians. Is there no danger for you?

To reveal the true nature of your faith, strip away your reliance upon family traditions, church attendance, church membership, or baptism. Look deeper than the pious words you say in the right company. Look beyond the well-intentioned assurances given by a trusted parent, pastor, or evangelist. Set these insufficient comforts aside and look at what is left. Then determine if you have what the Bible describes as genuine Christian faith.

After reading the Gospels through for the first time, a monk of the Middle Ages reportedly said, "Either these are not the Gospels, or we are not Christians!" Indeed, this is not a new problem, and it could be *your* problem.

FAITH
WITHOUT THE SPIRIT
Chapter 2

We have been enamored too long with our own sense of power, as if *we* held the key to eternal life. We do not. Salvation begins in the mind of God and is accomplished as His own work. Our discussion will reveal several kinds of faith experiences that do not at all correspond to the activity of God. True faith is a gift, not a tool for manipulating the Almighty (see John 6:44, Acts 13:48; 1 Corinthians 4:7; Ephesians 2:8-9; Philippians 1:29).

A day at sea in a small sailboat can be an exhilarating experience, an analgesic for frayed nerves. Imagine endless blue sky adorned with billowy clouds. The temperature is Caribbean. All is well. But you have not yet sailed the sea, and that is your express purpose for coming out. Hoisting your sail, you position yourself for the fulfillment of your cherished intention—to glide frictionless through the water. But nothing happens. Why? Simply this: There is no wind.

In the same way, it is possible to hoist the sail of what seems to be true faith even though no Wind ("Spirit" is *pnuema*, or "wind," in Greek) is blowing. Such faith is wasted, worthless.

To say that you have had what you call a faith experience does not in itself prove anything. Faith, after all, does not save; God alone saves, *through* faith. Faith is a necessary corollary, to be sure. You must believe if you are to be saved. But apart from the "wind" of God's Spirit, no one *can* believe. A hoisted sail has no power to make the wind blow; it only catches the wind when it does blow. Likewise, human decisions (often mistakenly viewed as certain evidence of saving faith) have no power to cause the Spirit of God to work.

> The wind blows where it wishes, and you hear the sound of it, but cannot tell where it comes from and where it goes. So is everyone who is born of the Spirit (John 3:8).

You can see this clearly in John 1:12-13:

> But as many as received Him, to them He gave the right to become children of God, to those who believe in His name: who were born, not of blood, nor of the will of the flesh, nor of the will of man, but of God.

Notice first of all that it is necessary to receive Christ for who He actually is. This is the essential doctrinal element of true saving faith— understanding and believing the biblical truths about Jesus without prejudice or distortion. This is what most first-century Jews refused to do.

He came to His own, and His own [that is, His own people, the Jews] did not receive Him (John 1:11).

In addition to understanding and believing the truth *about* Jesus, you must personally *trust* in Him in order to become His child. You must believe in such a way that all your hope for eternity is in Him alone! Yet apart from God's activity in you, you *cannot* believe in this way.

Your new birth as a Christian is not dependent upon your decision. This is plainly stated in John 1:13. Those who believe and become God's children are the ones "who were born, not of blood, nor of the will of the flesh, nor of the will of man, but of God" (also see James 1:18). If you are a child of God, it was *God's* decision.

You must believe . . . you cannot . . . but you will if God wills, and *only* if He wills. Paul confirms this when he concludes that salvation "is not of him who wills, nor of him who runs, but of God who shows mercy" (Romans 9:16). The Wind must be blowing.

The man with the withered hand illustrates this principle of faith (see Luke 6:6-10). Surely he had often tried to straighten out his hand on his own. Then Christ commanded: "Stretch out your hand!" He must stretch it out . . . yet he could not. But this time he did! Why was this experience different? This time *God* was involved. The man's faith did not prompt Jesus to heal him. His faith was the reasonable response to the activity of God. His healing began with God and ended with God. The

13

Wind was blowing. Though his experience was one of faith, he did not hold the key of faith until God granted it to him.

Dead men don't rise. Lazarus' body was decomposing behind the stone door to the crypt (see John 11). Dead men cannot hear. Yet Jesus commanded, "Lazarus, come forth!" He must . . . he could not . . . but he did!

Paul taught that all believers were previously dead in trespasses and sins. They were this way "by nature," just as the rest of fallen humanity. "But God, who is rich in mercy, because of His great love with which He loved us, even when we were dead in trespasses, made us alive together with Christ (by grace you have been saved) . . ." (see Ephesians 2:1-5). Spiritually dead people *cannot* believe. But note the words: "God . . . made us alive" (also see John 3:3; Romans 8:6-8; 1 Corinthians 2:14).

Take a covert look with me at four men who locked themselves in an abandoned warehouse, having stolen a key from the owner's key ring. They have all the drinks they need for a night of gambling around a rickety card table. One stark light hangs over the gambling arena. Profanity and liquor flow unrestrained. Then about 2:00 a.m. a loud shout is heard outside. "There's a fire in the building!" Uneasy glances are exchanged. But the instigator of the evening allays all fears by saying, "Don't worry, there's the door. We'll leave when and if it's necessary." Play resumes. Immediately the loud voice is heard again: "The door is locked!" Again there is uneasiness, to which the ring-leader responds, "Calm down men; I have the key," holding it arrogantly on display. A third time the voice is heard, "That key is defective. It locks the door but it will not open it from the inside!"

Hurriedly, the men push the table over, spilling their drinks on the ground. They rush to the door. Frantically trying the key in the lock, they find it does no good, just as the voice said. They pull on the handle until it breaks off in their hands. Cursing and screaming in panic, they repeatedly kick at the heavy door, to no avail. They are doomed.

If these men are to be freed, the person outside must pass the proper key under the door for their use. That one human savior happens to be the owner of the warehouse. He has been the subject of many slurs throughout the evening. The one they have made their enemy is their only way of escape.

Please do not think that I am saying by this illustration that faith is without due importance. God will not turn a deaf ear to genuine faith. The key of faith does open the door, just as the sail catches the wind. But that kind of faith—saving faith—is more a matter of God's activity in us than you or I have ever imagined.

It is not sufficient to conclude that you have had an experience that you call faith. Religious experiences don't save. Decisions don't save. God alone saves, through the faith He gives.

FAITH

WITHOUT CHRIST

Chapter 3

In India, it is still a custom, though perhaps a fading one, for parents to choose a mate for their child. Suppose the parents sign a contract for the marriage of their children, yet the young man and woman have never met. Suppose further that the meeting of these two for some reason never takes place.

Even though they have completed all the paperwork, there is certainly no marriage, for marriage is first of all a relationship. Marriage is not only a *contract*, it is essentially *contact*. This "knowing," fully consummated by the most intimate union, is not merely the ideal; it is marriage itself (see Genesis 2:24).

I fear that many in our churches only know the facts about the historical Jesus. But they have not been married to Christ as One revealed to them personally. These sincere professors of Christianity could not be His own sheep, for Christ has made relationship the essential issue:

> I am the good shepherd; and I know My sheep, and am known by My own (John 10:14).

Such self-declared Christians have willingly accepted the Christian concepts. They have endorsed the contract, but they have never come into marital affinity with Christ Himself. They must find out the truth: Knowing Christ and His Father is the beauty of true salvation and the content of saving faith.

> And this is eternal life, that they may *know* You, the only true God, and Jesus Christ whom You have sent (John 17:3, emphasis mine).

Those who are "christianized" without knowing Christ will be sadly disappointed at death, because life now and life later is summarized in knowing Him personally. "For to me, to live is Christ, and to die is gain," states Paul (Philippians 1:21). Though eloquently worded, that statement says nothing unique about Paul but affirms the testimony of every true believer. Knowing Christ now is what makes life *life*; to die and go to heaven is to know Him even better.

The list of New Covenant tenets in Hebrews 8 demonstrates that this knowing of Christ is experienced by *all* who are His:

> None of them shall teach his neighbor, and none his brother, saying, "Know the Lord," for all shall know Me, from the least of them to the greatest of them (Hebrews 8:11).

18

The writer of Hebrews has quoted an intriguing portion of Old Testament prophecy. Under the Old Covenant, most Jews did not know God personally. *Every* member of the New Covenant does.

All believers know Him. Yet "knowing" cannot be taught. No matter how much accurate and compelling information others could give you *about* Christ, there is still a large river you must cross. Knowing His biographical sketch accurately is not the same as knowing Him personally. This is not to dissuade you from seeking to know the facts. They are essential. But it plainly affirms the ultimate issue— *relationship*. Relationship is not just educational.

When the prophet Samuel was a boy, he "ministered to the Lord" (1 Samuel 3:1). Yet a few verses later we find this startling disclosure: "Now Samuel did not yet know the Lord, nor was the word of the Lord yet revealed to him" (verse 7). Are you like Samuel? Are you ministering before the Lord and participating in worship activities without yet knowing Him? If so, your faith is not valid for salvation.

At the heart of knowing is *communication*. God initiates that communication by "calling" us to Himself. Every true Christian is designated as one who is "called" (see 1 Corinthians 1:22-24; Romans 8:28-30; 9:22-25, etc.). "My sheep hear my voice," Jesus said succinctly (John 10:27).

Just as the Lord called Samuel, and revealed the word of the Lord to him, so God reveals Himself to believers today.

At that time Jesus answered and said, "I thank You, Father, Lord of heaven and earth, that You have hidden these things from the wise and prudent and have revealed them to babes. Even so, Father, for so it seemed good in Your sight. All things have been delivered to Me by My Father, and no one knows the Son except the Father. Nor does anyone know the Father except the Son, and the one to whom the Son wills to reveal Him (Matthew 11:25-27).

This will all come out at the Judgment. After passionate pleas from many religious but deluded people, Jesus will speak words that will shatter the last fragments of their hope: "I never knew you; depart from Me, you who practice lawlessness!" (Matthew 7:23). Jesus knew *about* them—indeed, He knew *everything* about them—but He did not *know* them. They never became one with Him. Faith without knowing Him and being known by Him will end like that. They will be cast out.

The principal way Christ reveals Himself is through His Word. When you see the Bible as not only true, but also immensely beautiful, excellent, authoritative, applicable, compelling, etc., then you are experiencing the work of the Holy Spirit in revealing the Lord Himself. This is God communicating. The person who says he understands the Bible, yet cannot honestly see it in these ways, is sadly mistaken. When Christ is revealed and understood, He is seen *as He actually is* and His words are heard *as they actually are*—beautiful, excellent, authoritative, applicable, compelling, etc. In fact, when God does this work it is irresistible. As Jesus said, "*everyone* who has heard and learned from the Father comes to Me" (John 6:45, emphasis mine).

In the same way that you might identify tearfully with a character on the pages of a book or in a movie—a person whom you have never met—you may have had an emotional religious experience when learning about Christ, and yet not know Him. You may even have expert knowledge about Him and still not know Him.

I urge you to ponder this: Is there communication? Do you know His voice? Do you recognize truth when you hear it? Do you understand and appreciate the unique authority and excellence of God's Word? Do you love Jesus Christ for who He is (not merely for what He gives) and long to be with Him forever? You have not really believed so as to be saved until you *know* Him in this way. Do not be deceived.

FAITH
WITHOUT REASON
Chapter 4

With all that has been said about faith being relational, I do not want you to think that we can throw
correct notions of truth out the window in ex-
change for experience. Faith is not a subjective
experience apart from fact. Faith is relational, but
it must also be rational It is not a matter of faith
being either subjective or objective; it is both.

Some say that you should espouse Christianity
even if there are few, if any, facts to substantiate
it. Facts are immaterial, they claim; a mere "Christ
consciousness" is all that matters. Who cares if
Jesus really did all of the things the Bible says He
did, or if He were actually born of a virgin and
raised from the dead? Experience Him subjec-
tively, and do not concern yourself with the details.

The widespread acceptance of this anti-rational
view, even in many churches, is greatly disturbing.
Faith is elevated above the facts of redemptive
history as if faith itself were able to save. Faith
cannot save apart from its biblical and historical
object—the divine person and saving work of Jesus Christ. Faith depends on truth, not upon itself.

Paul deals with this in an elaborate and logically powerful way in 1 Corinthians 15. He concludes that facts are not optional:

> And if Christ is not risen, your faith is futile; you are still in your sins! Then also those who have fallen asleep in Christ have perished. If in this life only we have hope in Christ, we are of all men the most pitiable (verses 17-19).

Yes, you may have faith, but that faith means nothing if it is not founded upon the facts of the historical death and bodily resurrection of Christ. Faith without the facts is futile.

Subjective experiences may also assume other deceptive forms. Once while returning from Europe I spent two hours discussing biblical Christianity with a foreign professor of international law who would soon be teaching at a major Ivy League university in the United States. He admitted that he believed in Christ, but not the Christ of the Bible who was literally raised from the dead. Appealing to the facts meant nothing to him. Yet his eyes watered as he told me of an experience in the nature of a supernatural "visitation" that assured him he was in touch with God.

Visions, dreams, spiritual impressions, bright lights, spirit beings in the room—these sorts of things convince many that they are joined to God. They have a sort of faith, but it has no relationship to the facts of history. The only "substance" is the experience itself. What is most amazing to me is the emotion such persons exhibit as they tell of their experience, and the absolute assurance that the experience has given them.

The Bible teaches that one may even receive another Jesus, another gospel, and another spirit (see 2 Corinthians 11:4). Such distortions are the work of the enemy who often uses persuasive and appealing religious leaders to convince the unsuspecting.

> For such are false apostles, deceitful workers, transforming themselves into apostles of Christ. And no wonder! For Satan himself transforms himself into an angel of light. Therefore it is no great thing if his ministers also transform themselves into ministers of righteousness, whose end will be according to their works (2 Corinthians 11:13-15).

You can be deceived. Your salvation depends on the facts of Christ coming in the flesh (see 1 John 4:1-3), dying for your sins (see Galatians 3:10-13), and being raised bodily from an earthly grave (see Romans 10:9; 1 Corinthians 15:1-4). Any faith in faith alone, even with a sprinkling of Bible words, or faith in a supernatural or emotional experience apart from the facts, is not valid.

FAITH

WITHOUT REPENTANCE

Chapter 5

Many who live in the United States are familiar with the caricature of the frontier preacher coming from the days of the Kentucky Revivals in the mid-19th century. The backwoods preacher is standing on a stump, waving his Bible and exclaiming, "REPENT!" while perspiration streams down his face. This portrait, interestingly, is not far from that of John the Baptist, whose voice also reverberated, "Repent, for the kingdom of heaven is at hand!" (Matthew 3:2). Jesus spoke these same words, as did all the New Testament leaders. Why the emphasis? Because they knew that unless a person's faith came by way of repentance it would only be wasted faith.

For a person to be *saved* (the word means "rescued"), would it not be necessary for him to realize that there is something from which he must be delivered? Christ did not come to bless good people, but rather to save sinners. He did not come to give people the added benefit of heaven attached to their already fulfilled lives. He came to snatch sinners out of the hellishness of their souls and deliver them from the hell of their destiny! Any other understanding makes too little of Christ's sacrifice.

Has your faith come out of repentance? I would never say that a person must be able to define repentance or even use the word at his conversion. Yet no one is saved without being repentant. Paul said that God "commands all men everywhere to repent" (Acts 17:30). It would take a deft theologian to exclude anyone from that command!

Compare your faith with that of the Passover celebrants in John 2:23-25.

> Now when He was in Jerusalem at the Passover, during the feast, many believed in His name when they saw the signs which He did. But Jesus did not commit Himself to them, because He knew all men, and had no need that anyone should testify of man, for He knew what was in man.

The startling significance of this passage is that the words "believed" on the part of the many, and "commit" on the part of Christ are actually the same word in the original language. They believed or trusted in Christ, but He did not entrust Himself to them! Why? Why this wasted faith? Because these were unrepentant "believers." They wanted to have Christ added to their lives—a wonderful and needed benefit. Who would not appreciate such miracles and excitement? And *everyone* was coming to Him. So they believed . . . but Christ knew their hearts. They were full of themselves, their religious pride, lust, anger, etc.

Is it not true that Christians can commit sins such as the above even after believing in Christ? Yes, but there is a significant difference in how a true believer comes to Christ. The repentant person comes *because* he is a sinner, desperate for deliverance from hell *and* from the sin that is dragging him there. The false believer also comes to avoid hell, but with essentially no desire for a thorough change from his life of sin. He may hate the consequences of sin, both earthly and eternal, but he has no true hatred of the sin itself.

Like the genuine Christian, the false believer may also experience a sense of comfort. The two may initially look alike to those around them. But they can usually be distinguished by what happens in the months and years after they believe.

Following his initial faith in Christ, the genuine Christian will display the fruit of repentance in his increasing rejection of sin and love of holiness. Many false believers, on the other hand, will eventually drop out of Christian pursuits altogether and return to their life of sin. Those who continue will often experience a measure of outward moral reform due to their association with Christians or other factors. They learn to repress their sinful behavior because it is unacceptable among the company they keep. But in their hearts, their affection for sin is unchanged. Their continuing love for sin may be cleverly concealed most of the time, even from themselves. But God sees the heart.

What is repentance? We find our best help in the exact lexical meaning of the word itself: "to change the mind." It is a profound change of mind (or heart) so closely associated with faith that we could call it the "prefix" of genuine faith.

"I see," you reply. "Repentance is *turning from sin.*" Yes, it is in a way, as will be seen, but not if you are implying that a person has the ability to behave acceptably before God prior to being indwelt by Christ. Repentance could never be a "work" required for salvation, for salvation is "not of works, lest anyone should boast" (Ephesians 2:9). Repentance proceeds from a change of nature that takes place in the heart. The same change of nature that causes a person to move from unbelief to faith also causes him to hate sin and love holiness. Repentance will inevitably produce a visible change, but it is ultimately a matter of the heart.

"Isn't repentance *sorrow for sins*?" you ask. No, not sorrow alone. There are many weeping over their sins this very hour, even in churches, who are no closer to conversion than was Esau sobbing over his lost blessing. However, having the right kind of sorrow does give us some clue as to the legitimacy of our repentance. Examine what Paul says about this matter in 2 Corinthians 7:10.

> For godly sorrow produces repentance leading to salvation, not to be regretted; but the sorrow of the world produces death.

Read the passage again: *Godly sorrow . . . salvation; sorrow of the world . . . death.* What is the difference between these sorrows? Four words turn on the light of understanding—"*not to be regretted.*" Let me illustrate.

A rich young man asked Jesus, "Good Teacher, what shall I do that I may inherit eternal life?" (see Mark 10:17-22). We would have immediately welcomed this man into the faith. He seemed so sincere and ready. We might have eventually chosen him for one of the boards or committees of the church. After all, he knew so much about how to handle money! But Jesus had a different view entirely. And therefore, He sent the young man away. Why?

Jesus knew what was in the man. There is no doubt that this respected citizen wanted eternal life. He did, but only to a point. What did Jesus know that others could not see? He knew the man had an idol in his life which he wanted more than life forever, more than fellowship with God, more than kinship with all the saints of history, even more than the riches of Christ Himself.

As in all that Christ said and did, He intended to impact this man in a way that would echo all the way down to our generation. So He intentionally asked for that one thing—the idol of his heart. "Go your way, sell whatever you have and give to the poor, and you will have treasure in heaven," He told the inquirer. "And come, take up the cross, and follow Me."

While many today would have led this sincere fellow in a "sinner's prayer" and affirmed him as a believer, Jesus demanded far more—a complete reversal of affections. This man could not live with such severity. He wanted eternal life, but not at the expense of what was life to him. He plainly could not come to Christ without the regret of losing all he loved. Barring a subsequent change not divulged in Scripture, his sorrow led him to hell.

So you see, the litmus test of this "change of mind" is the heart issue of regret.

What if the story had ended differently? What would the young man have told us about his inner motivations? I believe he would have said something like this: "Give up my possessions? At first I was shocked and angry, but I knew Jesus was right. Give them up? Gladly! They had become the biggest idol of my life. I had sold out my soul to them. It was not painful to be set free. I was relieved to give them up and follow Him!"

No one will come to Christ without sin. You come to Christ precisely because you *do* have sin. But you cannot come with the attitude of holding on to your sin. You may not say or secretly believe, as the young ruler found out, "I will come to Christ but will not relinquish that which is most important to me—my habit, my private life, my standing in society, my money, my independence, my own control." You come with your sin, but also with a deep desire to find deliverance from it.

It will be no surprise that the Spirit presses hard on your particular idol, the first love of your heart, for all you touch must become His. This is your "change of mind" and the true inward "turning from sin." Christ saves those who come that way, and no one else. So what about you?

THE INITIAL ACT OF FAITH

CHAPTER 6

Genuine conviction brings a person to the threshold of a repenting faith. Imagine a man trapped on the roof of a burning high-rise building, nearly overcome by smoke. His last thought as he fades into unconsciousness is that he has no hope other than to be rescued by someone else. He therefore places his entire confidence in the men in the helicopter circling above. Likewise, the person who is deeply convicted that sin has made him morally helpless and guilty before God is in a proper mindset for the Savior, Jesus Christ.

An unconscious man on top of a burning building can contribute nothing to his own deliverance. He is absolutely dependent on his rescuers. Likewise, the sinner who perceives his dilemma rightly knows he can do nothing to bring about his own salvation. Having no other hope, he will either despair or look to Christ for deliverance. There is nothing else he can do.

Jesus said, "Most assuredly, I say to you, he who believes in Me has everlasting life" (John 6:47). Such is the emphasis throughout the Bible. For example, the gospel account by John, the only complete book of the Bible written expressly for the purpose of leading people to faith in Christ (see John 20:30-31), uses the word *believe* or its modifications ninety-eight times. In the New Testament we find the word and its derivatives over 500 times.

One possible detour from saving faith is the misplaced dependence on a formularized prayer, normally called "the sinner's prayer." This is the way it is usually presented: "You must admit that you are a sinner and invite Jesus into your heart."

First of all, admitting that you are a sinner is not the same as repentance. Secondly, inviting Jesus into your heart is not a biblical prescription for salvation. To my knowledge, there is no such invitation in the Bible. Carefully consider Revelation 3:20 and John 1:12, because most who emphasize "the sinner's prayer" and "inviting Jesus into your heart" in their evangelism often quote these two verses. But I believe the context in each case conveys a different meaning.

The Spirit does indeed indwell every believer, and also places that believer in Christ (see Romans 8:9; 2 Corinthians 5:17; 2 Corinthians 13:5; Ephesians 1:13-14.). True Christians are joined to Jesus Christ in spirit (see 1 Corinthians 6:17). But even though Christ resides in the hearts of believers and they in Him, His entrance into the heart is clearly *not* the invitation of the gospel.

I have often heard people say something like this: "I know that I am a genuine Christian because I analyzed my experience and found that I did ask Christ to come into my heart. Since God promises to enter into the hearts of all who ask, and since I asked correctly and sincerely, I must be saved. After all, God doesn't lie." It is true that God does not lie, but that is not the issue. The question is not whether or not God lies, but whether you believe.

Any person who has faith will be saved whether or not he uses the words of the modern prescription. It does nothing to enhance the situation. Rather, it often confuses it. Be careful not to rely on any formula. Rely on Christ. No correctly worded prayer is an automatic door-opener to eternal life from God.

Interestingly, the only "sinner's prayer" found in the New Testament is "God, be merciful to me a sinner!" (Luke 18:13). Even without the wording of the modern formula, there was true repentance and faith in the heart of the man who prayed that prayer. Jesus knew, and approved, saying, "I tell you, this man went down to his house justified" (verse 14).

The faith that characterizes true believers is not merely a matter of saying or doing something once—going forward in church at the preacher's invitation, raising your eyes or your hand, "making a decision," "opening the door of your heart" or "inviting Jesus in." Many who now show none of the fruit of genuine saving faith made these types of commitments or "decisions" at some point in their past. Saving faith is an initial and ongoing belief in the truth about Jesus Christ (who He is and what He has done) and a lifelong reliance upon Him alone for salvation.

Let me illustrate what I mean by reliance upon Christ and how it begins:

Suppose my beloved old car needed repairs, so I asked you to give me the name of the best automotive repairman in the city. You highly recommended one particular man whom you and others considered the expert.

At your suggestion, I made the trip into the city to locate his shop. It was a quaint old place that had been in operation for over fifty years. I saw numerous certificates of training and letters of commendation on the walls, all of which made me more appreciative of your recommendation. When the man came inside where I was waiting, I pointed to my car and asked, "Can you fix this kind of car?" Without hesitating he replied, "Why, certainly. I know everything about them and I have all the parts in stock."

We stood there looking at each other awkwardly for a few unpleasant moments until the man asked, "Are you going to give me the keys?" "No!" I blurted out. "No sir, not at all. My father gave me this car and I am not about to trust you with it. I know what you 'experts' do with cars like this. You take out the insides and replace them with inferior parts. No sir, I'll not give you *my* car!"

The surprised repairman then made a profound observation: "Well, if you don't give it to me, I can't fix it."

Though no analogy is complete, this illustration does picture the nature of faith in its beginning. You must give your life to Christ in abandoned trust. Faith in its initial aspect is more like giving up than getting started. It is dismissing your own work as useless and depending entirely on Someone else's work to fix your inherent sin problem. True faith begins this way . . . and it continues.

Think about your coming to Christ. Have you come by trust in Him alone? More importantly, do you trust Him *now*?

So far I have placed before you four kinds of faith which are empty and worthless: faith without the Spirit, faith without Christ, faith without reason, and faith without repentance. I have also simply illustrated the concept of beginning faith in Christ.

There are two more counterfeits to consider.

FAITH

WITHOUT FRUIT

Chapter 7

I have a friend who was converted from a hard life on the streets. His experience was one of emotion and drama. Yet after watching his early steps, I wondered just how authentic his Christianity was. He continued to fall into sin after sin, yet with great remorse. Gradually a difference was seen, and the old life patterns faded out. Now more and more fruit has become apparent, and there is every reason to think of him as a genuine believer. He consistently finds joy in reading the Bible, spends his days thinking of how to respond under the Lordship of Christ, and has even had the rewarding experience of leading some friends into their own relationship with Jesus.

On the other hand, I have known many who started out with all the apparent signs of being a child of God. But where are they now? Their church attendance is all that speaks of a conversion. Can I be assured that they are in Christ? Not really, for there is nothing of Christ seen in them. They are essentially the same as everyone else, except for their custom of going to church.

Jesus said you can know a tree by its fruit. He went on to say,

> Not everyone who says to Me, "Lord, Lord," shall enter the kingdom of heaven, but he who does the will of My Father in heaven. Many will say to Me in that day, "Lord, Lord, have we not prophesied in Your name, cast out demons in Your name, and done many wonders in Your name?" And then I will declare to them, "I never knew you; depart from Me, you who practice lawlessness!" (Matthew 7:21-23).

Only the one "who does the will of My Father in heaven" will enter heaven. Jesus is not teaching that obeying God *makes* one a Christian. No, the way to Christ is by grace through faith. What He is saying so forcefully is that those who are His show the evidence of their salvation. They are like their Father. Only such persons will be free from condemnation.

Do you have such evidence?

This dramatic picture of the future is full of insight. See how sincerely these deluded church members will appeal to Christ. After all, they professed Him openly, they experienced the supernatural by performing great acts, beneficial acts, in His name.

The list is impressive: casting out demons, prophetic utterances, miracles! Though it is not mentioned in the passage, I am sure that other professing Christians will appeal to their own supernatural experiences: "Lord, I prayed and came out of the hospital alive! I must be a Christian!" "Lord, I prayed for that new car and got it! Surely I am one of Yours!" "Lord, You spoke to me in dreams!" But such appeals are based on that which is easily counterfeited—the supernatural. They forget that the most sinful men in town also dreamed dreams, and came out of the hospital alive, and are driving new and expensive vehicles.

You will not got the ear of God by appealing to supernatural experiences on the day when God will judge even the secret things of the heart. His holiness alone will drown out your most heartrending appeals until there is nothing left to say.

What is the fruit of the true believer? We may sum up the principal fruit of the Christian in one word: *love*—love for God, demonstrated by true affection for Him and obedience to His commands, and love for other people, seen in correct responses and good deeds. "Beloved, let us love one another, for love is of God; and everyone who loves is born of God and knows God. He who does not love does not know God, for God is love" (1 John 4:7-8). It is just that simple.

Jesus gave the right to the non-believing world to judge whether or not we are Christians by our love for each other. He said, "By this all will know that you are My disciples, if you have love for one another" (John 13:35).

This obedience, or fruit, is born out of the fellowship Christians have with God. Before becoming believers, we knew nothing of fellowship with Him. But now, because He first loved us, we love Him sincerely (see 1 John 4:19). We will do anything for the One we love. This fellowship motivates us, but His Spirit also empowers us. If you are a true believer, He "works in you both to will and to do for His good pleasure" (Philippians 2:13). Love is the fruit of the Spirit of God Himself (see Galatians 5:22-23).

This is the argument of 1 John. Its theme may be paraphrased like this: "If we say that we are one of His, yet do not display the fruit of a true believer, we are not one of His, no matter what we claim."

Read John's words regarding:

(1) *Love for God*

For this is the love of God, that we keep His commandments. And His commandments are not burdensome (1 John 5:3).

In this the children of God and the children of the devil are manifest: Whoever does not practice righteousness is not of God . . . (1 John 3:10).

He who says, "I know Him," and does not keep His commandments, is a liar, and the truth is not in him. . . . By this we know that we are in Him. He who says he abides in Him ought himself also to walk just as He walked (1 John 2:4-6).

(2) *Love for Others*

We know that we have passed from death to life, because we love the brethren. He who does not love his brother abides in

42

death. Whoever hates his brother is a murderer, and you know that no murderer has eternal life abiding in him (1 John 3:14-15).

If someone says, "I love God," and hates his brother, he is a liar; for he who does not love his brother whom he has seen, how can he love God whom he has not seen? (1 John 4:20).

And we also ought to lay down our lives for the brethren. But whoever has this world's goods, and sees his brother in need, and shuts up his heart from him, how does the love of God abide in him? My little children, let us not love in word or in tongue, but in deed and in truth. And by this we know that we are of the truth, and shall assure our hearts before Him (1 John 3:16-19).

These are just a sampling of the many passages on this principle in Scripture! No wonder James says that "faith by itself, if it does not have works, is dead" (James 2:17). It is impossible (as well as unbiblical) to imagine that a person who is a true believer will fail to act, in a substantial and increasing way, like his heavenly Father.

Believers living in a fallen world are sometimes entangled by its temptations. This is an unarguable reality. But for the Spirit of God Himself to regenerate and indwell a person, and yet leave his actions, words, and thoughts unaffected and unimproved, is an absolute inconceivability. Paul would say of such a person what he said of the Cretans: "They profess to know God, but in works they deny Him. . . . " (Titus 1:16).

43

Examine yourself. Christians produce a crop, "some a hundredfold, some sixty, some thirty" (Matthew 13:23). Do you have such a crop? Are you bearing the fruit of increasing holiness? Are you any different from your unbelieving friends? They might be peaceful, polite, dedicated to family, etc., but they do not at all love God. They violate even His most basic commands, such as "Seek first the kingdom of God and His righteousness," and "Do not love the world or the things in the world" (Matthew 6:33; 1 John. 2:15). Are you any different? Do you have any of the holiness of God to prove it? Or are you watching the same things, saying the same things, hearing the same things, desiring the same things, and doing the same things as everyone else?

Christian love is particularly evident when the believer is offended and, in the opinion of most, has every right to retaliate or become bitter. Persistent unforgiveness, however, should alarm the professing Christian, one who claims to be indwelt by the fullness of mercy Himself, Jesus Christ. If a person has received such mercy, he will be merciful himself.

> For if you forgive men their trespasses, your heavenly Father will also forgive you. But if you do not forgive men their trespasses, neither will your heavenly Father forgive your trespasses (Matthew 6:14-15).

If there is nothing of the actual character of God in you, but only the normal respectabilities of many who are without Christ, why not admit it and begin now to seek His mercy? Social respectability is not the same as holiness, and you are the one to lose if you do not know His mercy and grace. I know that pride, position, or reputation may hold you back. But will you forfeit everything good for the sake of your pride? Do not let a mistaken self-righteousness mask the true condition of your heart.

Imagine a young man who was greatly loved by his father and family. Soon he was off to college and into the business world, making quite a success of his life. He was considered a fine moral sort of man, with the world before him. Yet what others did not know was that he was completely rejecting the love of his father and the rest of his family. His father would call him, but he would not return the calls. His father would write, but he would throw the letters away. His father would offer to buy him a plane ticket to see the family, but he would not take it. By all outward appearances no one would doubt his integrity, yet he was committing the most serious of sins—the refusal to love.

You might appear in many superficial ways to be a Christian. But do you love God and the family of God in an evident way? Are you obeying His commands out of a heart of love? Are you responding correctly and benevolently toward others? Do you have sincere affection for your brothers and sisters in Christ? If not, your faith is in vain.

FAITH
THAT DOES NOT LAST
Chapter 8

In the tale, *The Pilgrim's Progress*, John Bunyan describes the journey of a man named Christian, a pilgrim on his way to heaven. The road he travels is filled with conflict and struggle. He faces the hill "Difficulty," the "Valley of the Shadow of Death," "Vanity Fair," "Doubting Castle," and an array of enemies to his faith, including Apollyon himself. Finally he reaches "The Celestial City." It is a story of the perseverance of genuine faith, from its beginning at the narrow "wicket-gate" all the way to heaven. What is most intriguing is that Bunyan wrote his allegory in 1676 while in jail in Bedford, England, because of his faith!

While on the journey to heaven, the believer has many apparent reasons for wanting to discard his faith. But the Bible teaches that God Himself will prevent this from happening. We may be "confident of this very thing, that He who has begun a good work in you will complete it until the day of Jesus Christ" (Philippians 1:6). You may stumble, even badly, but you will not ultimately fall away if you are an authentic believer no matter what the conflict, within or without. I deeply appreciate Peter's teaching on this.

> [God] has begotten us again to a living hope through the resurrection of Jesus Christ from the dead, to an inheritance incorruptible and undefiled and that does not fade away, reserved in heaven for you, who are *kept by the power of God through faith* for salvation ready to be revealed in the last time. In this you greatly rejoice, though now for a little while, if need be, you have been grieved by various trials, that the genuineness of your faith, being much more precious than gold that perishes, though it is tested by fire, may be found to praise, honor, and glory at the revelation of Jesus Christ . . . (1 Peter 1:3-7; emphasis mine).

In this stimulating passage, we find that believers are "kept by the power of God through faith." God, who created and sustains the universe, exercises that same power toward His own. No other power in all creation is great enough to pull the believer out of His protective grip (see John 10:28-29). He will preserve those who are His until the end. But He will not do so without the means of faith—the faith that He gives (see Ephesians 2:8; Philippians 1:29). Our faith must persevere, and God will see that it does. If your faith is a temporary faith, then it is not the kind of faith God has given and it will not stand the test.

Paul, the model of Christian endurance, described the experience of many in 1 Corinthians 15:1-2 when he wrote, "I declare to you the gospel . . . by which also you are saved, if you hold fast that word which I preached to you—unless you believed in vain." Do you have a faith that will "hold fast" or a faith that is "in vain"?

Compare the soils in Jesus' parable in Luke 8:4-15. The "seed" of God's Word falls on four types of soil. Three of these are descriptive of the non-Christian. The second soil in the parable, for example, is rocky and shallow. Jesus said, "But the ones on the rock are those who, when they hear, receive the word with joy; and these have no root, who believe for a while and in time of temptation [trial or affliction] fall away" (verse 13).

How like so many today who "went out from us, but they were not of us; for if they had been of us, they would have continued with us; but they went out that they might be made manifest, that none of them were of us" (1 John 2:19). One cannot always tell in the beginning if the soil is good or bad. But in time it will be seen that many who once professed to be Christians never had saving faith at all.

This will not be the case with true believers—those in whom God's seed has taken root in good soil. When the hot sun of affliction scorches them, they will "keep" the seed "and bear fruit with patience [perseverance]," "some a hundredfold, some sixty, some thirty" (Luke 8:15; Matthew 13:23).

The fact that true believers will persevere until the end, with tests and trials only making their faith stronger, gives us significant reason for rejoicing (see Romans 5:1-5; James 1:2-4, etc.). I was continually amazed at my own mother who died of the awful affliction called Alzheimer's disease. Alzheimer's is a degeneration of the brain cells resulting in the loss of proper use of the mind and ending eventually in the mind's inability to carry out even its life-sustaining functions. There is no known cure. Yet in the midst of it all, while experiencing all the normal confusion and difficulty of the disease, she clearly demonstrated perseverance in her faith. No, more than that, her faith intensified and she often erupted in praise!

She had saving faith—the kind that cannot be destroyed by trial but only purified. Yet there are many who never entered through Bunyan's "wicket-gate." Their faith was spurious. They appeared to have faith for a time, but they never had anything real. Jesus will say to them, "I *never* knew you!" (Matthew 7:23; emphasis mine).

The writer of Hebrews said, "For we have become partakers of Christ if we hold the beginning of our confidence steadfast to the end" (Hebrews 3:14). Those who are Christ's, he said later, are "not of those who draw back to perdition, but of those who believe to the saving of the soul" (Hebrews 10:39). Testing will help us to see if we are "of those who believe."

If you do not have *enduring* faith, you never had *saving* faith. Take a close look at your endurance.

WHAT MUST I DO?

Chapter 9

It is God who saves. Saving faith is an act of the will and a continuing state of trust in the revealed Lord, but it is His freedom to reveal Himself to whomever He wills (see Matthew 11:27; John 17:1-3; Romans 9:15-16). Saving faith rests upon the proper content of actual historical events and biblical truth (that is, the sinless life, physical death, and bodily resurrection of Christ, as well as His eternal existence as God who took on human nature through the virgin birth, etc.).

Saving faith is the required and reasonable response to the redemptive activity of God. God commands all people everywhere to repent (see Acts 17:30). His benevolent kindness should lead them to repentance (see Romans 2:4). It is unreasonable *not* to repent and believe. It is this fact, among others, that makes God just in condemning unbelievers (see John 3:18).

Saving faith is prefixed by repentance, or a thorough change of mind about sin and God. Saving faith is suffixed by affection for God seen in its fruit, obedience. Saving faith is evidenced by love toward others, both in terms of correct responses and benevolent deeds. Saving faith will endure, even though tested by fire.

Is saving faith the faith you have? What if you thought you were a Christian but were not? What if everyone else called you a Christian but you were not? What if friends said to you, "If I have ever known a true believer, you are one," yet you had never come to know Christ? What if you talked of heaven as your home while your destiny was hell?

The man or woman who finds no time or interest for discerning the counterfeit from the true is gambling at the highest stakes, and for keeps. Now that you have read most of this book, will you let the truth of it do its work?

What can you do? Here are some proposals I make on the authority of God's Word for those who doubt and those who may be deceived. Don't scan them lightly. Struggle with them until you have an assurance that is both biblical and unshakable.

1. Humble yourself before God. Ask Him to open your eyes to understand your condition. If you do not care to humble yourself and see which side you are on, you are revealing a state of inconsideration for the things of God, the usual sign of an unbelieving heart.

2. Admit your inability to properly understand your own heart. Confess that you could in fact be deceived, and that if you are blinded by "the god of this age," even your previously strong perceptions may be in error (see 2 Corinthians 4:4).

3. Be hard on yourself in applying the evidences of true and false conversion to your own life (see 2 Corinthians 13:5; Luke 13:24; 2 Peter 1:5-11). If God's Word says believers display a particular action or attitude and unbelievers another, then be honest in admitting which description fits you best. The book of 1 John is a good place to begin.

4. Carefully examine the relational aspect of conversion—knowing Christ. Pursue intimacy with Him (see Philippians 3:7-11). If you know Him at all, you can know Him better, which will be a great assurance to you. If you cannot know Him better, you have never known Him at all. Cultivate a life of prayer and meditation.

5. Look for the fruit of love in your life—toward God and man. Do you have fellowship with God? (see 1 Corinthians 1:9; 1 John 1:6). Do you see the evidence? Examine the fruit by first removing the surface considerations: your habit of church attendance, your use of christianized language, or your dependence on an experience. Is love there? Ask God to give you discernment to recognize the difference between the love of the Spirit and a mere natural affection. Love is displayed in . . .

> • *Affection and Obedience Toward God*
> Is your love for Christ greater than all your other loves? (see Matthew 10:37; 16:24-25). No one may rightly expect perfection in this life, but increasing obedience to Christ is one indicator of true love for Him and therefore, true conversion (see John 14:15, 21, 23-24; 1 Corinthians 16:22). If there is no change for the better, no altering of your affections, and no improvement

53

in your character, then you are not a believer, no matter what you may have thought (1 John 3:7-10). Distinguish between obedience to God's commands and man-made legalism. Look at your inner motivations.

• *Affection for Believers*
Do you love other Christians? (see John 13:34-35; 1 John 4:20-5:1). Are you drawn to spend time in fellowship with them? Do you share a spiritual bond with them—one that is even closer than you have with unsaved family members or friends? (see Mark 3:31-35; Matthew 10:34-37).

• *Responding Biblically to All*
Study 1 Corinthians 13 and seek to apply the attitudes and responses of love to see if you have been given grace to do them. If you are unloving by persistently holding a grudge, your bitter heart reveals the absence of the Holy Spirit (Galatians 5:19-23). Unforgiving people are unforgiven people. To be unforgiven is to be damned (see Matthew 6:12, 14-15; Matthew 18:21-35; Romans 12:17-20). The ability to show genuine love even toward your enemies indicates that "you will be sons of the Most High. For He is kind to the unthankful and evil" (Luke 6:35).

• *Doing Good Works*
The heart of a Christian should overflow with love for others. He is like his Master who "went about doing good" (Acts 10:38). Seek ways to do good to Christians and

non-Christians alike (see Ephesians 2:10; 1 Thessalonians 4:9-10; Galatians 6:10). Jesus distinguishes between those who carry out good works and those who do not; one group goes to hell, the other to heaven (Matthew 25:31-46). "But whoever has this world's goods, and sees his brother in need, and shuts up his heart from him, how does the love of God abide in him?" (1 John 3:17; also see Romans 2:5-10).

6. Evaluate your response toward God during testing. Is your faith purified through such experiences? Or have you been able to forget God and go on with your life? Have you become angry at God for what He has brought into your life? Seek now to respond correctly to testing, but be honest in examining the depth or superficiality from which your responses spring If you are able to respond well, you will assure yourself as to your state (see 1 Peter 1:6-9). If you often do not respond well to testing—if trials make you distrust God or become angry with Him, or if they cause you to drop out of Christian pursuits emotionally or physically—then you are not a believer (see 1 John 2:19; Matthew 13:20-21).

7. Trust the living Christ unconditionally. Have no other hope for eternal life than Him. Transfer any trust in your own "good works" or supposed merit over to Christ alone (see Ephesians 2:8-9). Trust Him now. Invite Him to inspect and test the authenticity of your faith so that it may be exposed or strengthened. A strong faith is a strong assurance; a weak faith is a weak assurance; a false faith is a false assurance (see Hebrews 11:1). Keep before

your mind that saving faith is responding to the revealed Lord, not "gritting the teeth" and convincing yourself you are saved.

8. Plead for mercy (see Luke 18:13; Ephesians. 2:4; 1 Peter 1:3).

In our day of instant food, lightning-fast communication, and thirty-minute plot resolution on television, it is hardly conceivable that one would suggest serious reflection on anything for more than an hour. Before God, I plead with you to forsake any kind of surface examination. At this precise moment in hell, church members once as respected as you are recounting in agony the opportunity that was lost. Some may be your relatives and friends. They would give the entire world, if they owned it, for even a moment on earth to think about it once again!

For every second you live here, billions upon billions of years will be spent in eternity. If thinking this through is of no importance to you, then you are hopelessly insensible. I have wept for people like you. Even the faintest awareness of the existence of a final state of judgment, with its unbearable suffering and complete hopelessness, should wrench the emotions of any normal person. Surely those who cannot grieve over their fate in the light of such certainties are the abnormal ones of our world.

But sadly, some of you will place this book on a bookshelf or in a drawer and go on unwittingly to your destiny. Only later will you have time to think—only when it is too late.

Therefore, brethren, be even more diligent
to make your calling and election sure,
for if you do these things you will never stumble;
for so an entrance will be supplied to you
abundantly into the everlasting kingdom of
our Lord and Savior Jesus Christ .

2 Peter 1:10-11

A FINAL NOTE

The Bible addresses the assurance of salvation in two ways: First, we look *away from* ourselves to Christ and His life, death, and resurrection on behalf of sinful people. Second, we look *at* ourselves to see if God has given us spiritual life. The first emphasizes what the Bible calls "justification" (that all who come to God by faith in Christ are accepted as righteous before Him because of who Jesus is and what He did, though they are sinners); the second emphasizes "regeneration" (that all believers have received visible and discernible life from God Himself). *Wasted Faith* is a close look at the second of these.

For a basic but thorough explanation of the gospel, with an emphasis on justification, read *Pursuing God—A Seeker's Guide*, by Jim Elliff. This, and other resources, may be found at
www.CCWtoday.org.

A *Wasted Faith* discussion guide for small groups and mentoring is available online as a free download.

Seek the Lord while He may be found,
Call upon Him while He is near.
Let the wicked forsake his way,
And the unrighteous man his thoughts;
Let him return to the Lord,
And He will have mercy on him,
And to our God,
For He will abundantly pardon.

Isaiah 55:6-7

Christian Communicators Worldwide

CCW is a ministry based in Parkville, Missouri, a "river-stop" town in the Northland of the greater Kansas City area. We enjoy this quaint town with its beautiful park, interesting shops and eateries, and the stately Park University which overlooks it all. The meandering Missouri River, navigated by Lewis and Clark on their expedition, runs along the south end of the town. Independence, Missouri, the starting place for the Oregon and Santa Fe trails, is not far from Parkville. There is a lot of history here at "the beginning of the Westward advance."

Like those who explored and settled the western regions of the United States, CCW is also on a mission—to extend the message of Christ as far as God will allow. We do that through our websites (see next page) and through the speaking ministry of our founder, Jim Elliff. We also do this through Jim's writing ministry and that of his assistants, Daryl Wingerd and Susan Verstraete. CCW publishes books and booklets, offered by us and by other booksellers. Tens of thousands of pieces of free literature have also been distributed, both here and overseas.

Please visit our web sites:

www.CCWtoday.org
This is our main site, with numerous articles, ministry tools, audio messages, and information about ordering our publications.

www.WaytoGod.org
This site contains articles and audio designed to guide interested people into a relationship with Jesus Christ. Here we also answer questions from inquirers.

www.BulletinInserts.org
This site provides timely and instructive bulletin inserts, handouts, and tracts. We offer free, downloadable inserts (also available in A4) for every Sunday of the year.